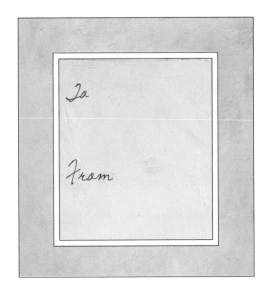

To

From

Flavia ®

Birthdays Are Gifts
copyright © 1993 by Flavia Weedn
All rights reserved. Printed in Hong Kong.

No part of this book may be used or reproduced
in any manner whatsoever without written permission
except in the case of reprints in the context of reviews.

For information write
Canadian Greeting Card Corp., Ltd.
P.O. Box 2517, Station 'A' London,
Ontario N6A 4G9

ISBN: 0-8362-4713-2

BIRTHDAYS
ARE GIFTS

Written and Illustrated
by Flavia Weedn

Life

is a

miracle

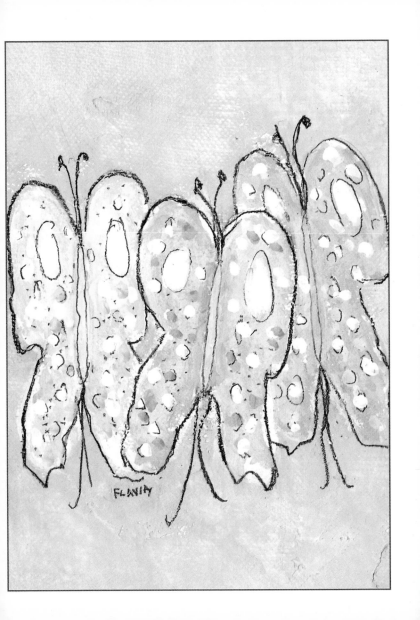

and

birthdays

are gifts.

Each

year

comes

wrapped

FLAVIA

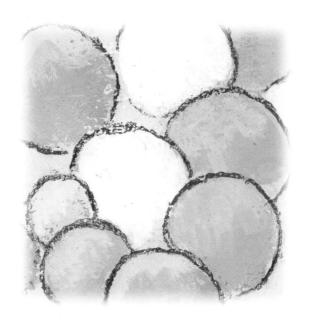

in

a ribbon

of dreams...

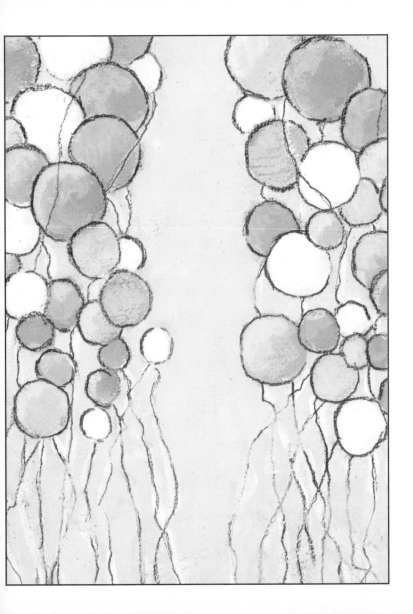

and

whether

you

are

very young

or very old

or

somewhere

in

between

*life is
filled with
wonderful surprises.*

So

when

you

stand

beside

your

cake

FLAVIA

may

you hear

the wish

I make...

a wish

that your

birthday

wish

comes

true.

Happy
Birthday

Flavia at work in her Santa Barbara studio

Flavia Weedn is a writer, painter and philosopher. Her life's work is about hope for the human spirit. "I want to reach people of all ages who have never been told, 'wait a minute, look around you. It's wonderful to be alive and every one of us matters. We can make a difference if we keep trying and never give up.'" It is Flavia's and her family's wish to awaken this spirit in each and every one of us. Flavia's messages are translated into many foreign languages on giftware, books and paper goods around the world.

To find out more about Flavia write to:
Weedn Studios, Ltd.
740 State Street, 3rd Floor
Santa Barbara, CA 93101 USA
or call: 805-564-6909